MACK MODEL AB
PHOTO ARCHIVE

MACK MODEL AB

PHOTO ARCHIVE

Photographs from the
Mack Trucks Historical Museum Archives

Edited with introduction by
Thomas E. Warth

Iconografix
Photo Archive Series

Iconografix
P.O. Box 18433
Minneapolis, Minnesota 55418 USA

Text Copyright © 1994 by Iconografix

Library of Congress Card Number 94-76265

ISBN 1-882256-18-2

94 95 96 97 98 99 00 5 4 3 2 1

Cover and book design by Lou Gordon, Osceola, Wisconsin

Printed in the United States of America

Book trade distribution by Voyageur Press, Inc. (800) 888-9653

PREFACE

The histories of machines and mechanical gadgets are contained in the books, journals, correspondence and personal papers stored in libraries and archives throughout the world. Written in tens of languages, covering thousands of subjects, the stories are recorded in millions of words.

Words are powerful. Yet, the impact of a single image, a photograph or an illustration, often relates more than dozens of pages of text. Fortunately, many of the libraries and archives that house the words also preserve the images.

In the *Photo Archive Series*, Iconografix reproduces photographs and illustrations selected from public and private collections. The images are chosen to tell a story—to capture the character of their subject. Reproduced as found, they are accompanied by the captions made available by the archive.

The Iconografix *Photo Archive Series* is dedicated to young and old alike, the enthusiast, the collector and anyone who, like us, is fascinated by "things" mechanical.

ACKNOWLEDGMENTS

The photographs and illustrations appearing in this book were made available by the Mack Trucks Historical Museum. We are grateful to Colin Chisholm, Curator, for his assistance.

A comparison of 1918 and 1924 models showing the larger radiator, as introduced in 1923. April 1924. (M17182)

8

INTRODUCTION

"Built like a Mack Truck" what a wonderful statement—one of the best descriptions you can give to a piece of equipment designed to stand up to tough conditions. Since just after the turn of the century, Mack has been turning out trucks of such a quality that the phrase has become part of our language. The first truck placed in the Smithsonian Collection was a Model AC—the venerable "Bulldog".

The Mack brothers first made their name as horse drawn wagon builders in Brooklyn, New York in the 1800s. About 1902 they produced their first motor vehicle, a sightseeing bus powered by a 24 horsepower 4-cylinder engine. It was so successful that business grew and they looked for a new plant. Allentown, Pennsylvania was chosen as its site, and Mack Brothers Motor Car Company was set up. It was here that the brothers produced their first trucks, which ranged in size from 1-1/2 to 5 tons. Later, larger trucks up to 7-1/2 tons were built.

By 1911, Mack were producing over 500 trucks a year, and were generally recognized as the largest truck manufacturer in the country. However, this activity needed capital. To gain the support of bankers, the brothers joined forces with the distributors of the Swiss Saurer truck and the Hewitt Company to form the International Motor Company. The new company manufactured the Saurer truck under license, certain Hewitt models, and an increasing number of Mack models. Growth quickened but financial problems continued and two of the Mack brothers left the company.

The outbreak of World War I changed the fortunes of Mack. It was at this time that the AB or "Baby Mack" was introduced, a modern, medium-duty truck designed by E. R. Hewitt. The AB was an advanced looking vehicle for its time, and between 1914 and 1936 nearly 52,000 units were built. While the shovel-nosed AC or "Bulldog", which was sold in basically the same years as the AB, undoubtedly is more famous, the AB sold in larger numbers. It was on these two models that the long term success of the company was built.

As introduced in 1914, the AB was offered in 1, 1-1/2, and 2 ton sizes. Power came from a 30 horsepower 4-cylinder gasoline engine. In the first models, many of the parts were made by outside suppliers. As the line got into its stride, Mack manufactured the whole vehicle. Worm drive was standard, until replaced by double reduction drive in 1920, and chain drive was available as an option in all but the first year or so. An early AB catalog indicates a top gear speed of 17 mph. Wheelbases of 132 and 144 inches were available on the 1 ton chassis; 144 and 162 inches on the 1-1/2 and 2 ton chassis. Fuel consumption of between 9 and 10 miles to the gallon was promised.

The hood line of the AB changed significantly in 1923 with the introduction of a larger radiator. A year earlier a dropframe chassis had been introduced for bus bodies. By 1927, load capacities were 1-1/2, 2, and 2-1/2 tons, with wheelbase options of 146-1/2, 164 1/2, and 182-1/2 inches, 200-1/2 and 218-1/2 inches available by special order. In the later years sizes up to 6 tons were offered. Engine size was 251 cubic inches in the 1-1/2 ton and 284 cubic inches in the larger trucks. In the 1930s, a 6-cylinder engine was available in the AB, and for the last three years of production the AB cab was similar to that of the later pre-war B models.

Mack Model AB Photo Archive presents an exciting cross section of photographs selected from the Mack Trucks Historical Museum. They are presented in a roughly chronological order and largely without editorial comment. Negative numbers are included when known. Captions on factory photographs in the early days were sparse, but we hope that by presenting these fascinating early images the reader will be encouraged into further research.

Allentown Plant Number 1, home of the Model AB. (V1102)

The first AB prototype featured worm-drive. Photographed at the 64th Street plant, New York City. Spring 1914. (H47)

(H222)

(H243)

14

2 ton and 1 ton chassis. (H300)

Right and left side views of the Mack 4-cylinder engine. 1914. (H45)

(H46)

Chassis with Apelco dynamo and lighting system. 1914. (H138)

2 ton, right-hand-drive chassis. 1914. (H143)

Dump truck on a 1915-1916 worm-drive chassis. (K124)

20

(M15657)

2 ton AB. (H371)

22

A coal delivery truck on a 1916 AB chassis. (M17162)

1 ton AB. 1915. (752)

(H401)

The frame and chassis of a prototype World War I armoured car (never put into production). (504)

ARMORED CAR
MOTOR CO NEW YORK

(H556)

2 ton AB owned by Standard Aero. (K856)

Electric light and trolley wire repair tower wagon. (K503)

U.S. government field trials in New York City. Circa World War I. (H726)

(H732)

(H573)

A 1916-1919 1-1/2 ton worm-drive chassis with year around cab. (780A)

(H167)

34

(H326)

A 1915-1918 worm-drive chassis with Mack Brothers-type cab and wooden wheels. (K226)

Worm-drive, 2 cubic yard dump truck. Seattle, Washington. (K374)

(K526)

38

2 ton AB. (H341)

(H562)

40

Standard Oil Company tanker on a 1915 AB chassis. (K230)

A bus body on a 1917-1920 chassis (before introduction of the special bus chassis). (M17116)

(K1603)

1919 worm-drives. (M17231)

A fruit-type body on a 2-1/2 ton chassis. Chicago, Illinois. 1915. (M17232)

(K1608)

46

An express-type body on a 1918-1920 dual reduction 1-1/2 ton chassis. Chicago, Illinois. (M17178)

Three section, electrically operated tower wagon used for repairing street lights. Milwaukee, Wisconsin. (K2399)

A paddy wagon, belonging to the Charleston, South Carolina Police Patrol, on a 1920-1922 1-1/2 ton chassis with special fire department motor. (M17138)

Four 1916-1919 worm-drives. (K1792)

50

A fruit-type body on a 1918-1920 dual reduction 2-1/2 ton chassis. Chicago, Illinois. (M17177)

(K1976)

52

Bottle trucks on a 1919 worm-drive chassis. Savannah, Georgia. (M17234)

(K2300)

(K1725)

(K2597)

56

A 600 gallon gravity sprinkler on a 2-1/2 ton chassis, convertible into a 2 yard dump truck in winter. Borough of Neptune City, New Jersey. (K3016)

A van body on a 2-1/2 ton chassis. Bridgeport, Connecticut. (K2424)

(K831)

A 1918-1920 AB chain-drive tractor. (K2778)

A 3 cubic yard dump truck, with double acting tail gate, on a dual reduction 2 ton chassis. (K2485)

An AB with Lee Line Hoppers. (K3020)

A 3 cubic yard special refuse collection body on a 2 ton chassis. New York City. (K2393)

A 2 cubic yard dump body, with double acting tail gate, on a 2-1/2 ton chassis. Town of Fallsburg, Sullivan County, New York. (M17174)

(K2956)

Chassis and dump body in branch showroom. (1661)

Front and rear sprocket and chain of an AB chain drive chassis, showing Mack high nickel-chromium cast-iron brake drum bolted to forged and casehardened rear sprocket; also showing front sprocket of forged, casehardened steel. (A6949)

(K1434)

68

162 inch worm-drive chassis. (860)

Dual reduction drive was introduced in 1920 to replace the worm-drive. (K2203)

(K2202)

A 1919-1920 AB Caterpillar-type Roadless tractor. (K3916)

AB Roadless tractor being tested by government officials. December 1922. (K3973)

(A1302)

74

2 ton AB. (711A)

(A1300)

1923 New Look

1923 saw the end of the "small radiator" period. Experience had shown the need for increased cooling capacity for the Baby Mack, and so a larger radiator using tubes and fins was introduced. This changed the whole appearance of the truck, as the radiator stood proud of the hood line. The neatness of the earlier hood line was lost and the appearance became more utilitarian. Apart from trucks on the AB bus chassis, this style continued through to 1933, at which time a more modern cab was introduced. The new cab was almost indistinguishable from those used on some of the pre-war Model B Series.

1926-1927 period. (526)

146-1/2 inch wheelbase chassis with dual reduction drive and larger radiator. (A1589)

An insulated ice cream body with hinged doors in the roof for filling compartments with ice and brine. Norfolk, Virginia.

Special cab for bus chassis. September 1925. (A2017)

(A1639)

(9125)

Filling in a mine breach. Summit Hill, Pennsylvania. September 1927.

Richfield Oil Company tankers. Oregon. October 1928. (L2521)

(L2633)

November 1928. (L2655)

(L2689)

(L2765)

(L2705)

(L2706)

(A3337)

February 1929. (A3009)

February 1929. (A3008)

July 1929. (A3409)

April 1928. (A2554)

March 1929. (A3890)

100

Detail of power take-off for line truck application. October 1929. (A3552)

Flat body on a 2-1/2 ton, 200-1/2 inch wheelbase chassis. Weight 9090 lb. September 1928.

Dump trucks belonging to the King County Road District No. 2, Seattle, Washington. June 1929. (L3499)

(L3318)

May 1929. (L3327)

May 1929. (L3328)

Road oiling equipment on a 2-1/2 ton, 175-1/2 inch wheelbase chassis. Weight 12,200 lb. May 1928.

October 1929. (L3818)

Radio Oil Company tanker. Massachusetts. September 1930. (L4999)

Richfield Oil Company tanker on a 2-1/2 ton, 164-1/2 inch wheelbase chassis. Weight 11,430 lb. May 1928.

Tanker bearing the name of Standard Oil Company of New York written in Greek. (L4065)

Line of oil tankers on AB and AC Bulldog chassis. March 1929. (A3107)

Van body with bus type radiator and California steel wheels. Weight 10,860 lb. October 1929.

(L3924)

(L4531)

South Bend "Suburban-type" street flusher on a 2-1/2 ton, 164-1/2 inch wheelbase chassis. Town of Miami, Arizona. Weight 10,600 lb. March 1929.

Stake body on a 200-1/2 inch wheelbase chassis. Los Angeles, California. Weight 10,750 lb. December 1928.

Stake body on a 2-1/2 ton, 182-1/2 inch wheelbase chassis, with overload springs and Budd wheels. Weight 10,200 lb. April 1929.

Line trucks belonging to Lehigh Telephone Company, Lehigh, Pennsylvania. June 1929. (A3305)

AB chain drive chassis. March 1930. (A3876)

Newly available 6-cylinder engine in an AB chassis. April 1930. (A4008)

September 1930.

124

Street grading in Allentown, Pennsylvania. August 1930.

Left and right side views of the Mack 4-cylinder engine. December 1931. (A4937)

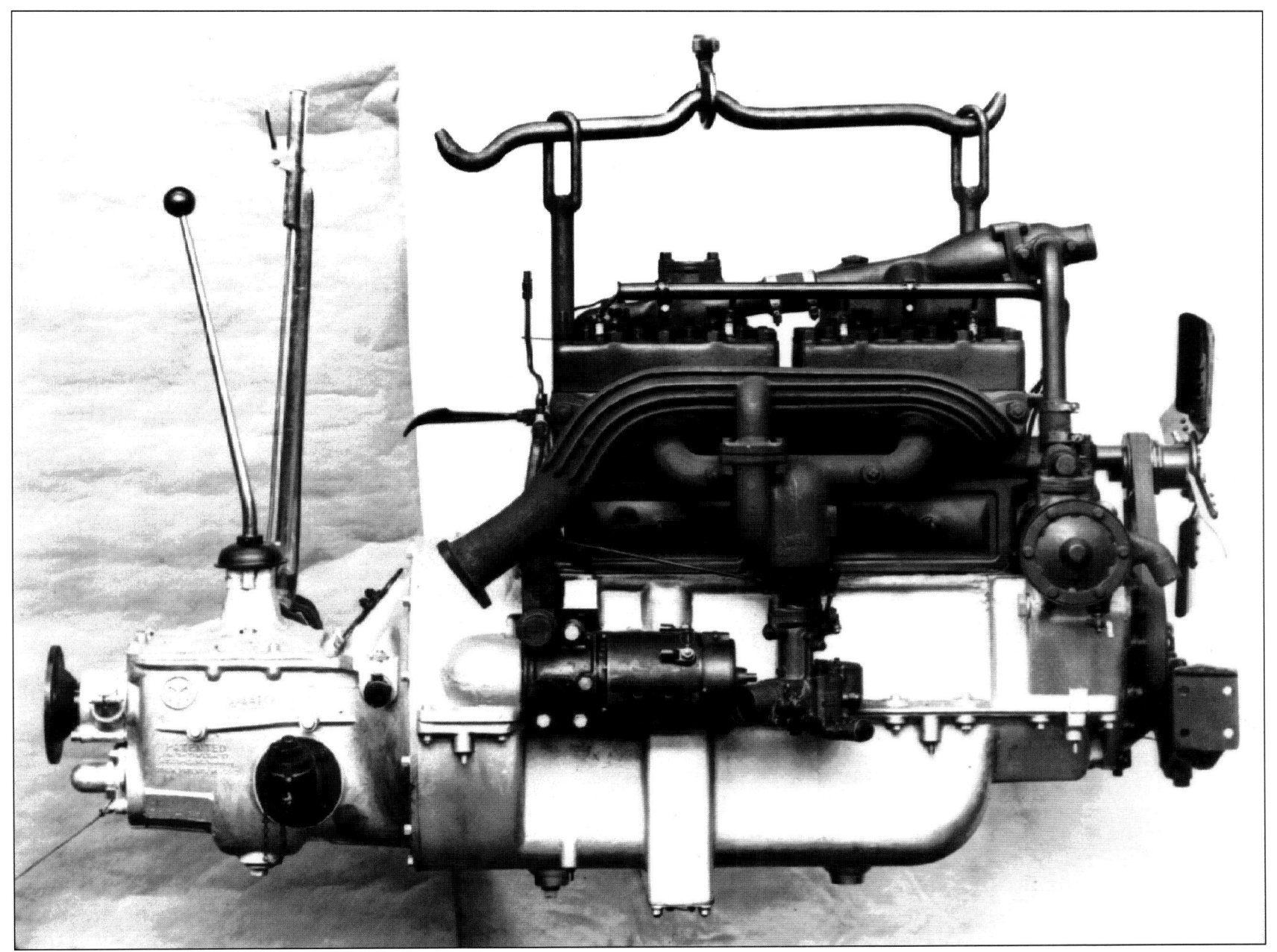

(A4938)

Beverage truck (capacity 168 cases) sold to Marion Coca-Cola Bottling Company, Marion, South Carolina. June 1932. (L6029)

A line of beverage trucks on AB chassis (first truck on the right is not an AB). New Orleans, Louisiana. March 1931. (L5339)

Beverage truck on a 2-1/2 ton, 164-1/2 inch wheelbase chassis with 4-cylinder engine. Weight 9,940 lb. 1930.

Dump truck on a late AB chassis. February 1932. (A4988)

Milk truck on a dual reduction chassis with 4-cylinder engine. Milk Producers Association, Stockton, California. July 1934. (M619)

(M567)

A Model AB photographed in Minnesota in 1954. (M17101)

Dual reduction chassis with 4-cylinder engine. Seattle, Washington. July 1934. (M621)

Interior and overhead views of a Mack deluxe cab on an AB 4-cylinder chassis. August 1934. (A6055)

(A6059)

Oil tanker mounted on a 196 inch wheelbase bus chassis. October 1934. (5960)

Ale and beer delivery truck on a 1935 AB chassis. November 1935. (M1343)

Jaeger concrete mixer on a 153-1/2 inch wheelbase chassis with Budd wheels. Weight 20,120 lb. March 1935. (1088)

BIBLIOGRAPHY

Montville, John B., *Mack*, NJ, Walter Haessner, Inc., 1973.

Montville, John B., *Mack, A Living Legend of the Highway*, Tucson, AZ, Aztex Corp., 1979.

Rasmussen, Henry, *Mack, Bulldog of American Highways*, Osceola, WI, Motorbooks International, 1987.

The Iconografix Photo Archive Series includes:

JOHN DEERE MODEL D Photo Archive   ISBN 1-882256-00-X
JOHN DEERE MODEL A Photo Archive   ISBN 1-882256-12-3
JOHN DEERE MODEL B Photo Archive   ISBN 1-882256-01-8
JOHN DEERE 30 SERIES Photo Archive   ISBN 1-882256-13-1
FARMALL REGULAR Photo Archive   ISBN 1-882256-14-X
FARMALL F-SERIES Photo Archive   ISBN 1-882256-02-6
FARMALL MODEL H Photo Archive   ISBN 1-882256-03-4
FARMALL MODEL M Photo Archive   ISBN 1-882256-15-8
CATERPILLAR THIRTY Photo Archive   ISBN 1-882256-04-2
CATERPILLAR SIXTY Photo Archive   ISBN 1-882256-05-0
TWIN CITY TRACTOR Photo Archive   ISBN 1-882256-06-9
MINNEAPOLIS-MOLINE U-SERIES Photo Archive   ISBN 1-882256-07-7
HART-PARR Photo Archive   ISBN 1-882256-08-5
OLIVER TRACTOR Photo Archive   ISBN 1-882256-09-3
HOLT TRACTORS Photo Archive   ISBN 1-882256-10-7
RUSSELL GRADERS Photo Archive   ISBN 1-882256-11-5
MACK MODEL AB Photo Archive   ISBN 1-882256-18-2
MACK MODEL B, 1953-66 Photo Archive   ISBN 1-882256-19-0
          Available Fall 1994
CATERPILLAR MILITARY TRACTORS
  Photo Archive, VOLUME 1   ISBN 1-882256-16-6
CATERPILLAR MILITARY TRACTORS
  Photo Archive, VOLUME 2   ISBN 1-882256-17-4
LE MANS 1950: THE BRIGGS CUNNINGHAM
  CAMPAIGN Photo Archive   ISBN 1-882256-21-2
SEBRING 12-HOUR RACE 1970 Photo Archive   ISBN 1-882256-20-4

The Iconografix Photo Archive Series is available from direct mail specialty book dealers and bookstores throughout the world, or can be ordered from the publisher.

For information write to:

Iconografix   Telephone: (715) 294-2792
P.O. Box 609   (800) 289-3504 (USA and Canada)
Osceola, Wisconsin 54020 USA   Fax: (715) 294-3414